CHOPPING without CHOPPING:
micrologues

Judith McNally

Copyright © 2012 Judith McNally
All rights reserved.
ISBN: 1470034247
ISBN-13: 9781470034245

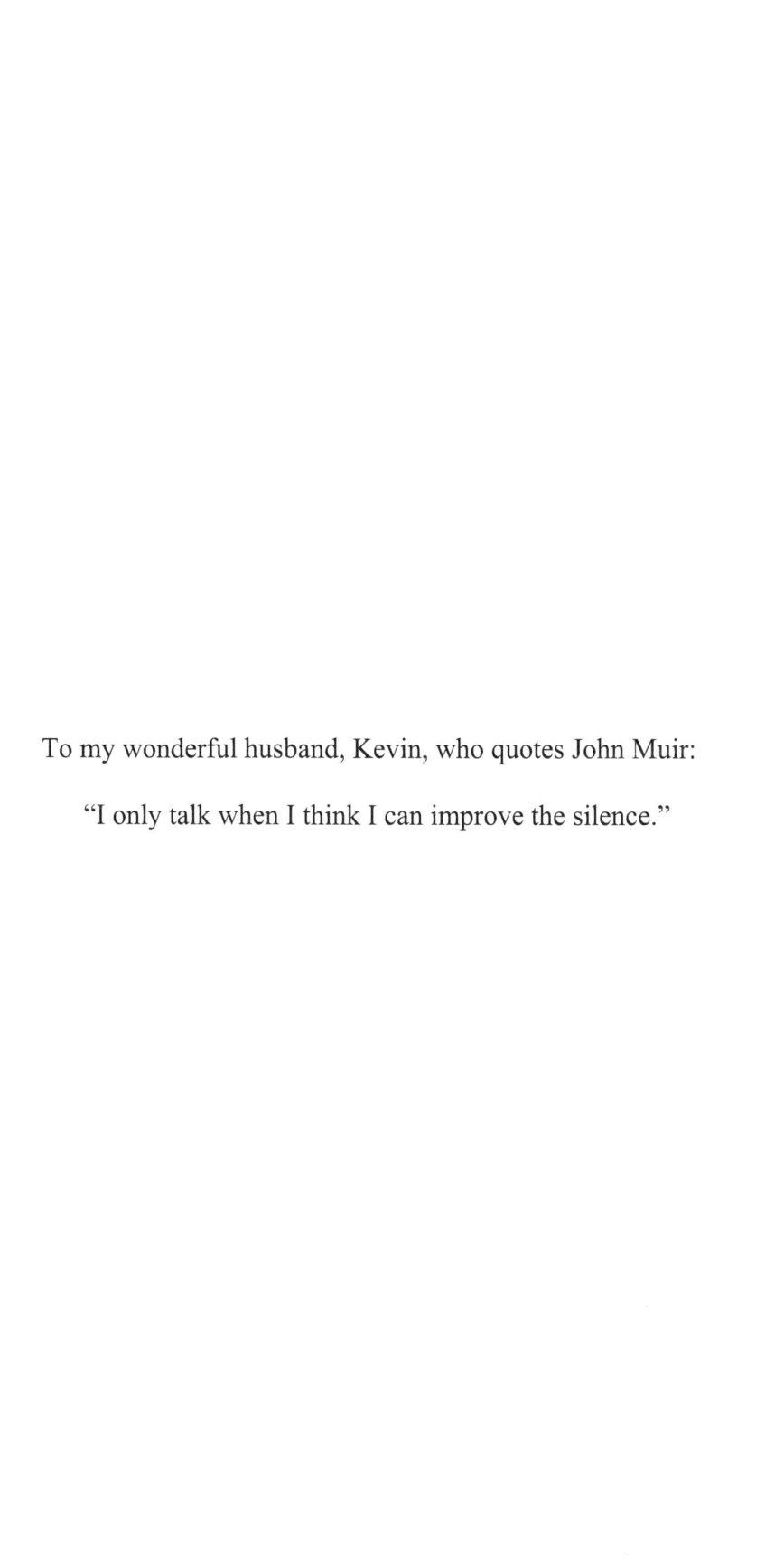

To my wonderful husband, Kevin, who quotes John Muir:

"I only talk when I think I can improve the silence."

INTRODUCTION

These short dialogues are meant to be read as non-gender specific pieces for any two people. These "micrologues" are fun to read to yourself, aloud with a friend, or for practice with a fellow drama student.

I started writing these as an antidote to people who were trying to make me into a flapping ear. As one older friend said, "A conversation ought to go back and forth like a ping pong ball."

Over time the micrologues grew to be a way for me to think things through, sometimes in lieu of a journal entry. When I taught Creative Writing, to adults, college students, and in high school residencies, the dialogues came to be about how closely we do – or do not – listen to one another.

The characters here, denoted simply as "A" and "B," are different for each micrologue. There are very few markings as to intonations; it is hoped that the lines will speak for themselves.

I'm indebted to Tricia Fagan, who coined the term, "micrologues," for these.

Grateful acknowledgment is made to the poetry journals, U.S.1 Worksheets and Thatchwork, for publishing "Here and Now" and "Chopping without Chopping," respectively.

Thanks also to Liz Parker, who brought together actors for a reading at the Cheryl King Studio, NYC.

J.M.

November 2011

The Collection

HERE AND NOW

A   When do you lose the present moment?

B   The present moment?

A   Yes. What distracts you?

B   How would I know if I was in the present?

A   Nothing would be distracting you.

B   From what?

A   From the present.

B   But how would I know?

A   You'd be focused.

B   On what?

A   The here and now.

B   This conversation, for instance.

A   Yes. Unless your mind is wandering as we speak.

B   Then wherever it wanders to is the present.

A   No.

B   If I'm thinking I have to buy cat food, then that's my focus. That's my present moment.

A   But the conversation isn't about cat food.

B   It is now.

A   The cat food is a distraction.

B   From what?

A   From the question about what distracts you.

B   That's the present moment for you. Why do I have to be in your present moment, instead of you being in mine?

A   Well, for starters, I don't have a cat.

B   Couldn't a conversation shift from your original question, over to cat food?

A   Shifting and wandering are two different things.

B   It's still one person controlling what the conversation is about.

A   Well, it's sort of a contract that two people enter into when they have a conversation, that they're going to talk about the same thing.

B   Have you ever thought about having a cat?

A   No, but—

B   Because they can be very affectionate and independent, both.

A   I—

B   And cats are very in the moment. Even when they stare at something, and you look, and there's nothing there.

A	Right.

B	So even cats get distracted. Unless they're hunting. Then the focus is absolute.

A	Maybe I should be having this conversation with your cat.

B	Maybe when he wakes up.

##

REMOTE CONTROL

A   What are you saying?

B   There's a remote control that can control humans.

A   A remote?

B   Yes.

A   How?

B   It sends signals to the ear. It can make you dizzy, or make you fall.

A   Is this for the military?

B   There's talk of it, as an alternative to killing someone.

A   But that's not the primary purpose?

B   I think it's for video games.

A   So the news would sound something like, 'Insurgents in Baghdad were reported dizzy today.'

B   The device can also make you move left or right.

A   So it could jerk your hand in a voting booth?

B   No one mentioned that.

A   Or make you reach for a certain cereal in the supermarket? Or direct an artist's hand?

B   I think you're talking science fiction.

A   Today's fiction; tomorrow's realities.

B   You'll give people ideas.

A   Isn't there some way to resist the device?

B   You can cling onto something, but then you can't move at all. Anyway, it could help the elderly from falling.

A   Aren't there some ethical issues here?

B   That depends.

A   On what?

B   On who markets it first.

##

THE WAITING GAME

A   What are you doing?

B   Waiting for the phone to ring.

A   As least it's concrete.

B   Compared to what?

A   *"Waiting for Godot"*.

B   I just went through my nihilist phase.

A   Oh?

B   I encountered the great void of nothingness, got scared and ran like hell before the earth gave way and I went tumbling in.

A   I see you made it.

B   Yes. But I'm still waiting.

A   There's no need, with a cell phone.

B   Psychologically, I'm still waiting.

A   It must be a very important call.

B   It's just the next thing on my agenda.

A   What about multi-tasking?

B   You mean, do something else while I'm waiting.

A   Yes.

B   The something else would only get partial attention.

A   That's in the nature of multi-tasking. The attention flickers from one thing to the next.

B   It dilutes the concentration.

A   It's demanding.

B   I go on my own way, one thing at a time.

A   A luxury, these days.

B   Computers only do one thing at a time; they just do it very fast.

A   Multi-tasking speeds things up, that's for sure.

B   The idea is to turn humans into computers? We already have computers. We need humans to be human.

A   You can't change the pace of the Information Age. It's either sink or swim.

B   Well, I suppose I could pick the dry leaves off the begonia while I wait.

##

PORTUGAL

A   I've done my chores and errands. Now what?

B   Something to save the world.

A   Such as?

B   Or something you enjoy. If you're lucky, they're the same thing.

A   Such as?

B   I don't know. Give someone a compost bin. Weave a lovely scarf. There are probably as many ways to save the world as there are people. Maybe you could just smile.

A   In this day and age? It would count as suspicious behavior.

B   No one's ever been arrested for smiling.

A   I know someone who lost a job because he smiled too much.

B   What was it – a funeral home?

A   Something financial. Price Waterhouse. People like you to be serious when it's about money. I once sold charter flights to Europe. People didn't like it if I joked around.

B   Did you go?

A   To Europe? Yes. But only because one couple cancelled out at the last minute. It was their honeymoon. They couldn't get a refund. So technically, I sold enough seats that I could go.

B   You went on someone else's honeymoon?

A   Technically, yes.

B   What were your favorite memories?

A   There were oranges on the trees in Portugal. And the almond trees were in bloom

B   You were focused.

A   I bought a fishermen's cable knit sweater, from the woman who knit it.

B   Do you think being focused in the moment makes for sharper memories later on?

A   I remember when I had an ice cream cone this summer.

B   I mean as a theory, in general.

A   It was black raspberry.

B   Maybe people could get along better if they had better memories.

A   It was very good.

B   I meant if the memories were sharper.

A   People tell me I have an excellent memory.

B   Then use it.

A   For what?

B   Saving the world.

A	How?

B	Tell us the good times – and the bad – but tell it so the mountain tops can hear it as it echoes in the valleys. Tell it gently, like dew drops on a spider's web. But most of all, tell it with clarity, in an open envelope, for all to hear. Let it rest upon your shoulder, waiting, for its time.

	##

MYSTIC

A   She's a what?

B   A cleaning lady.

A   But she's a Harvard Ph.D. She did her thesis on Rumi.

B   She needed a job.

A   But that's absurd!

B   To eat is absurd?

A   A cleaning lady? Where?

B   A department store. The night shift. She says it's quiet.

A   Rumi was a mystic. What's so mystical about a quiet department store?

B   She can feel his presence.

A   Which department store is this?

B   Target.

A   Where is he – among the silk flower candle rings, or the hair ribbons?

B   She says she doesn't mind. She doesn't have to publish anything, and she doesn't have to put all the commas in the freshmen compositions.

A   Was she planning on this when she got her degree?

B   No. Actually I think she had her mind set on J.C. Penny's.

                                                                ##

A MYTHOLOGICAL EXPERIENCE

A   We stopped off at these American Indian mounds. And right away Mike is practically in a trance. I didn't feel *any*thing. Later he said he had a metaphysical – no, mythological experience.

B   Did he say what?

A   I didn't ask. He spent practically the entire rest of the day writing in his journal. And then when it was his turn to drive, he didn't say anything, either.

B   That's unusual – for Mike.

A   So I don't know whether it was intensely private, or if he needed the time to think about it.

B   A mythological experience.

A   There was a perimeter mound, about twenty feet high, and then on the ground, there was a six foot-high mound that branched off into three parts. That's where Mike had his experience. I looked at them and thought, oh, this is nicely cared for, and isn't it lovely the way the mounds look like a bird in flight. But that was as far as I got.

B   People have different experiences.

A   Do you think something was calling to him? Or maybe he already had this idea in his head. I don't mean to belittle it, I'm just—

B   Jealous.

A   Yeah.

##

EAST-WEST

A   Ever wonder what the East coast is doing?

B   East coast of what?

A   New York. Maine.

B   What do you mean?

A   I feel so 'ahead of the times' out here.

B   Why?

A   We're so Earth-conscious.

B   And what – in New York they pour the East River over their pancakes?

A   You don't get the feeling out here that we're the pacesetters? What we do, they do?

B   I haven't been here that long.

A   You'll see.

B   I think the question is more like what are they doing on the East coast of China, or Africa.

A   I didn't know you were so global.

B   I read the papers, I make my lunch and then I'm at work. I go to the gym. I have a few friends. Once in a blue moon I go to a party. I like to walk in the part and feed the squirrels.

A   How long have you been out here?

B   Six months.

A   Are you seeing anyone?

B   Does that mean do I have a girlfriend, or a therapist?

A   I mean because we could go out.

B   You and me?

A   Yes.

B   I wasn't expecting you to – I thought we were just—

A   Do you want to think about it?

B   No. Actually I'd like to.

A   O.k. Because I mean I've been out here three years and sometimes I feel like I hardly know anybody. Everybody's so busy, you know – saving everything.

                                                                                    ##

TREE

A   I don't think you should do this.

B   You don't?

A   I don't think you're ready.

B   No?

A   It's too much of a stretch for you.

B   This is a relief.

A   For who?

B   For me.

A   This is news.

B   I didn't want to say.

A   What were you waiting for? I mean, if I hadn't happened to say anything, you were going to rush headlong ahead?

B   I don't think so.

A   No?

B   I think I would have put on my own brakes. I would have just known, not to go ahead.

A   How?

B   Oh, the right tree. A bird. Maybe a cloud.

A   What is this – like Elvis sightings?

B   Very funny.

A   As long as you know what you're doing. I mean, I don't always get the impression you realize this is your *life* you're dealing with.

B   I'm careful.

A   I just don't want a bluejay to fly into your life and that suddenly means you move to Nova Scotia.

B   There are no jobs in Nova Scotia.

A   I know that. Just so *you* know that.

B   No. I'm like a fruit tree. I'll grow, and then it will be a while before there's any fruit.

A   I'm waiting with you, kid.

B   I need that.

A   As long as it takes.

B   Right.

A   And don't get astrological on me, either. O.k.?

B   I already did that. I'm the local train that makes every stop.

A   And don't hurry. Me, I have this very strong feeling that I have to hurry like crazy to catch up for all the mistakes I made. But you, take your time. Grow. Be a good tree.

##

CLAIRE

A   In my wildest imagination, I never thought I'd see you again.

B   Here I am.

A   I almost used to pray I wouldn't.

B   Like I said, here I am.

A   What are you doing here?

B   Came back to haunt you.

A   No.

B   It's a big world. The chances of us meeting are something like three billion to one.

A   Is this my lucky day?

B   Does that mean we go out for a bite to eat? I just got off the plane. I'm starved.

A   Didn't they feed you?

B   I'm watching my cholesterol.

A   It took a lot for me to get over you. It's not exactly a scab I'd like to tear off.

A   Nine years?

B   I spent four of them letting go. While you, obviously, went whirling around the world without even looking over your shoulder.

A   You're sure about that?

B   When Harry Left Sally. Yes, I'm sure.

A   I didn't know you felt that way.

B   You never asked.

A   I heard bitter. I don't go to lunch with bitter.

B   Seeing you again – it's bringing up a lot.

A   I recognized you from a block away. Did you watch the Oscars? You always watch the Oscars.

B   Did you?

A   I had work to do.

B   Liz Taylor was on.

A   I caught that part.

B   Nothing's changed.

A   With me? Sure.

B   You still only tell one tenth of yourself until someone drags more out of you.

A   I'm a big boy. I can eat lunch by myself.

B   I have to get back.

A   It was good seeing you. I mean that.

B   Three billion to one.

A   And I'll tell you something I never told you.

B   What?

A   I think of you.

B   Bye.

                                                    ##

BLINK

A   Anyway, it's not enough.

B   Of course it is.

A   We won't get further than Chicago on this.

B   Then Chicago it is.

A   I want ocean.

B   There's the Great Lakes.

A   We should have sold the exercise bike for twice that.

B   Everywhere's the same.

A   No.

B   Pretty much.

A   Not south Texas and Vancouver. New York and Livingston, Montana.

B   The people, I mean. If they're friendly.

A   And if they're not?

B   Then they need food, water, encouragement.

A   Spare me the social worker line.

B   But that's what I did. That's how I got through.

A   But you're still like that. Sunshine sprouting between your teeth.

B   Not a bad way to be.

A   It's not realistic.

B   You want the enamel to peel off my teeth? That's realistic?

A   I heard that salt water taffy is very good for teeth.

B   You're really set on ocean?

A   A little house by the shore.

B   Oh – now we're talking real estate!

A   And sand castles. I don't care if they wash away. To build them – that's enough.

B   They have contests.

A   No. Me and the taffy and the roar of the waves. This is all I ask.

B   What happened to the hang glider?

A   I sold it.

B   You didn't even ask me, and it's gone? Who bought it?

A   A young couple. Said they were looking for adventure.

B   What did you tell them?

A   About the time I blinked and almost – no, I didn't tell them about that. They seemed so thirsty. Almost…

B	Almost what?

A	The way we were. I mean, would we have listened? Would we? So I sold it to them, and you could see them already moving that way, holding on, the balance, the absolute concentration that gets you so high, and I couldn't tell them, that all I wanted to do now was build sand castles and concentrate that same way, only now, it would be a grain of sand. Do you know what I mean?

##

THEORY & PRACTICE

A   I knew him from grad. school. I remember saying to him once that having an affair sounded good in theory, but that in practice it would tear his relationship apart.

B   Did he listen?

A   They moved to California. He was station manager for a tv station out there. He wrote. Once.

B   What did he say?

A   He said, 'How did you know?'

                                                  ##

LANDING

A   You couldn't take any more of it.

B   No.

A   Like a dragonfly landing. That light. That heavy. And that sudden.

B   What are you going to do now?

A   I don't know.

B   You have to pay the rent.

A   My Aunt Margaret does that.

B   Forever?

A   Long enough.

B   I used to wonder why I never saw you scuffling. What's it like?

A   You remember that time I went to India?

B   For a year.

A   I came back and there wasn't anybody to play with. Everybody works. Sometimes I wish I did, too.

B   At what?

A   Maybe a community garden. For kids. Blind people. Retired. Anybody. Prisoners.

B   The fertile land of the imagination. Why don't you start one?

A   Which – a garden, or an imagination?

B   You could.

A   You're so earnest.

B   What's wrong with earnest?

A   It takes away that layer where the dragonfly lands. Light. And sudden. I have to go now.

B   Where?

A   Nepal.

##

BONES

A   Any time you waltz with me, I'm blooming like gardenias! Any time you waltz with her, I'm full of wrath and crackling bones.

B   What are crackling bones?

A   When a person gets so angry they crack their own bones.

B   You heard this?

A   No. I made it up. It means I get jealous.

B   There's no reason.

A   No?

B   You waltz better than anyone on the floor – cracklin' bones and all.

A   Momentary comfort.

B   And the gardenias won't be out for months. You're ahead of your time.

A   Is that why you won't marry me?

B   I won't marry you because I can't keep up with you.

A   I could slow down.

B   No. We'll dance now and then, and call to one another over the fields.

A   Go on – the next dance is starting.

##

OLD TIMES

A   You coming?

B   I don't know.

A   I'm going.

B   Why?

A   Old times.

B   I don't have any of that.

A   Everybody has old times.

B   Not like you.

A   I'm not so different.

B   Most people go on.

A   With what – stone hearts?

B   Don't go pointing any fingers at me.

A   But to look at you.

B   What – the clothes?

A   That smile you have.

B   I found it by the roadside, reflecting off some hubcap.

A   Thought you said it came from inside.

B   My real smile?

A   Yeah.

B   Buried that years ago.

A   Why?

B   Made me look too starry-eyed.

A   What's wrong with starry-eyed – if it's the real you?

B   Looks like I haven't been around.

A   So?

B   Otherwise you get taken advantage of.

A   You mean it's all a cover?

B   Call it anything you want.

A   So are you coming or not?

B   No. I'm going to sit right here and forget about the old times.

A   Suit yourself. I'm going.

B   To see the old rocker?

A   Garden, brook, house, the porch. The old rocker, yeah.

B   Forget it.

A   Still holding a grudge, aren't you.

B   Don't I have reason?

A   After this long?

B   Don't I have reason?

A   Just as well go up and rock some, yourself. See how good it felt.

B   Never said a word. Just rocked and rocked.

A   'Cause he was at that point where he didn't have to.

B   What about when I told him I was leaving? He could have said *some*thing.

A   Yeah. But he didn't have to.

                              ##

PAINTING THE TOWN RED

A   It's one of those rainy days – the kind they tell you to save up for.

B   Did you?

A   Did *you*?

B   Hell, if I did, I don't know it. Lived every day like it was the last drunken brawl on earth. I been down, I been up. You don't want me to tell you the story of my life, now do you.

A   Better than thinking about mine.

B   All the guy did was walk out on you.

A   That's all? My life is in shambles.

B   Nah. It just needs a little dusting around the corners. Tell you what. You get yourself fixed up, get those red eyes washed out, and we'll go out on the town.

A   I don't want to go anywhere.

B   I know it. But believe you me, it's the best thing for you.

A   You don't understand. I *hurt*.

B   Oh, I know. Believe me, I know. Now you go on in there, fix yourself up.

A   He just left half an hour ago. Don't you have any respect for the dying?

B Nobody dying *I* can see. Now I'll tell you what. I'll take myself outside on the porch, set a spell. And when you get done, you come on out and I'll be there. Ain't I always been there for you, ever since you were born? Would have married you myself, if it wasn't for me being old enough to be your uncle twice removed.

A You would have?

B Now you go on. Set a spell. Cry, if you need to. Clear the air. I'd just as soon shoot up the bastard, myself – him leaving you like that. Go on now. I'll be outside. You take your time.

A Uncle George?

B Yes'm?

A I'd just as soon see this town tonight.

##

A BIG WORLD

A   It can't be.

B   You have another explanation?

A   I don't have *any* explanation.

B   Unless of course you believe in miracles.

A   What do you think?

B   What I said.

A   It makes no sense.

B   So?

A   Forget logic. Forget synchronicity. Forget everything in between.

B   What's in between?

A   I don't know. Censorship. Darwin. Good will.

B   That's your continuum?

A   I told you. I'm too distracted to think.

B   Do you want to go over the details again?

A   I've *been* over them. What I want is an explanation.

B   Maybe there isn't one.

A   Sherlock Holmes giving up?

B   No. Ordinary person shrugging their shoulders and going on.

A   You can do that?

B   I just did.

A   Where does that leave me?

B   Lacking in shoulder exercise.

A   C'mon. I'm serious.

B   It's a big world out there. Things happen.

A   The cosmos sends messages.

B   It's more like a wave at the ocean. You let it carry you. Then you stop worrying how far out from the shore you are. It feels good.

A   I'm still back at the breakers.

B   I have to go now. You'll be all right?

A   Me? Yeah. Just here with whatever it is. I'll be all right. Just, uh, when you leave, shut the door tight?

##

THE OTHER BOX

A   What's that box there?

B   Which box?

A   That one.

B   Oh – *that* one.

A   Yes. What's in it?

B   You want to know what's in it?

A   Yes. Or can I just open it?

B   Now?

A   Is there some reason I should wait?

B   I don't know yet.

A   What is it you don't know?

B   Whether you're the one to open the box.

A   The one? The one to open this particular box? What's in it?

B   All the goodness in the world.

A   All the goodness- - !?

B   You asked.

A   You mean this box is the exact opposite of Pandora's box, with all the evil in it?

B   You asked.

A   So why are you waiting to open it? You could stop all the wars, and all the famine, and sickness and –

B   Hold your horses.

A   Why? How could you?

B   We haven't found any one person who can handle the responsibility.

A   What about Ghandi, or Martin Luther King, or Madame Curie? Or Louis Armstrong?

B   They're all dead.

A   I see…

B   Are you still interested in the position?

A   (hesitating) Can I get back to you?

##

SALAD DAYS

A   That your garden?

B   Yes.

A   New one, looks like.

B   Just starting.

A   What are you planting? Carrots, looks like. Lettuce. Broccoli. What else have you got in there?

B   Tomatoes.

A   I can see that. Take care of your fertilizer? Very important, fertilizer.

B   There's a horse farm nearby. I went there.

A   Good, good.

B   I take it you're quite the gardener, yourself.

A   Me? Oh no, no. The wife used to have one.

                                                       ##

JUNK

A   What kind of junk is this?

B   What do you mean, 'junk'?

A   It falls apart, you step on it, you get ashes.

B   No.

A   I made the real stuff. Don't I know what junk is?

B   It isn't what you think.

A   A horse isn't a horse. Right? This is junk!

B   Grandpa, listen.

A   You bought this? For good money? Nobody even knows anymore what is the real thing. They should be ashamed, buying junk!

B   Grandpa, not everyone can afford handmade wrought iron.

A   Who can waste their money on junk? My grandchildren should know what comes from *work*. Does a machine know what it means to work? Does a machine sweat? Does a machine get calluses that last a lifetime?

B   Grandpa, I don't run this world – I only inherited it.

A   Didn't I offer to teach you?

B   Who shoes horses in Chicago?

A   Railings. I could have taught you. Safe railings so your mother won't fall down.

B   She takes the elevator. What's to hold onto?

A   In my day, there were railings. None of this talk, these crazy workshops you go to, looking, searching for something to hold onto. *Railings*.

B   It's a little more complicated now.

A   It was always complicated.

B   The world is converging now. Pretty soon there will be no such place as Ethiopia. There will be Earth, and people who spend more time or less time on soil and concrete where there used to be an Ethiopia. Or China. Or us.

A   Maybe I should take a workshop – learn how you people put up with all this junk. I don't. Can't stand a day of it. Jennie, bless her soul, must have died of it. Pancreatic cancer – ha! It was junk, I tell you. Don't know why it hasn't got me.

B   Grandpa, would you like to take a walk? The dogwoods are out.

A   Ought to make stuff like they make trees. Solid. Last a hundred years.

B   Do you want your sweater? I don't want you to catch a chill.

A   I don't need a sweater. Show me the way. Always did like a good dogwood. Graceful little cups, curving out. Hard to make a good curve. Why wouldn't you let me teach you? Just like your father –had to forge your own way.

B   It wasn't what I wanted to do, Grandpa. I *like* working on the Stock Exchange. All that hustle and bustle suits me.

A   Did my father give me a choice? At first I said no – I was going to be a farmer on my own land – but am I any the worse for being a blacksmith?

B   It won't be light out much longer, if we're going for a walk.

A   Always did like twilight. Jenny and I used to stroll down the lane, arm in arm. Used to wonder at her touch – so gentle through my rough hands. Those bellows pumping all day, eyes fastened on that glowing iron. And there was your grandmother in my arms, sweet as a day could be. Memories. That's all that's left. And junk.

##

BAMBOO

A   Somewhere there's a cloud waiting for me. All I have to do is find it, straddle it, and ride on away, heidi ho-ho.

B   Where to?

A   The nearest raindrop. Then I scoot down, grab a change of clothes and take the next moonbeam up to heaven.

B   You have a rather adventurous agenda.

A   At my age, you don't have time not to.

B   What is it you do once you get up to heaven?

A   Stay there, of course. Moonbeams don't come along everyday.

B   This helps you, does it? To cope?

A   Dearie, there hasn't been a day all my life I didn't shed a tear for *some* corner of the Earth. But the forsythia are out, I have my bamboo to saw up for tomato stakes, and did you ever look at how the bamboo tip wraps around itself in layers? There's a little point at the tip of each one, with two smaller points alongside. Will you take a look at that!

                                                           ##

THE PLEDGE OF ALLEGIANCE

A   Do they still say the Pledge of Allegiance in schools?

B   Of course! Where have you been?

A   When you don't have kids, you don't know these things.

B   It was prayer they omitted.

A   I was only wondering how global the children are getting, and if they now said, 'I pledge allegiance to the Earth.'

B   How can you pledge allegiance to an Earth that's still fighting with itself? 'I pledge allegiance to Earth including the Khmer Rouge'?

A   There could be a start, anyway. A kind of universal pledge in Swahili as well as English.

B   People would wrangle for years over what it would say.

A   A kind of peace and environmental pledge.

B   Think of the committees!

A   Then let the children write it.

##

THAT ONE RUNG

A   Why are we doing this, anyway?

B   I don't know.

A   Then it doesn't make any sense.

B   Maybe it wouldn't make any sense even if we did know.

A   I can't buy that.

B   It makes no difference if you do.

A   Then what do you hang on to?

B   Either nothing, or faith – your choice.

A   What is this – the lottery?

B   You could look at it that way.

A   What do I get if I win?

B   As I said – nothing, or faith.

A   I have to buy a ticket every day?

B   That depends.

A   On what?

B   How much faith you want – or how much nothing.

A   I didn't know it was a game of chance.

B   Well, you don't necessarily get as large a return as you'd hoped for. But that's not the point.

A   What is?

B   What Gary Cooper said – to look like you can always take care of yourself.

A   Gary Cooper said that?

B   Yes.

A   How do you take care of yourself based on nothing?

B   I'm not the person to ask.

A   Then for you, it's faith.

B   Yes.

A   And you play the lottery every day.

B   It's more like an insurance policy that never runs out.

A   Insurance, lottery. Next you'll say mah jong.

B   It isn't so easy to explain. It's like what we're doing here – bouncing cups and plungers off a drum. Maybe it doesn't make any sense, but—

A   But what?

B   But it feels richer than doing anything else. And maybe that's as much as a hold as we ever get on anything. That one rung, to hold onto.

##

SPIES

A   This is strictly the last time.

B   What do you mean?

A   There are government spies everywhere, and you insist on putting out your newspaper. Don't you know when to quit? I said I'd help. Here I am. This is the last time. What do you want me to do?

A   Calm down.

                                                                   ##

TWO FRIENDS

A   Sometimes, the bird flies off. Doesn't come back for days and days. Other times, it never leaves its perch. Remarkable, don't you think?

B   Where do you suppose it goes?

A   Oh, I don't know. Just off. Do you mean, put one of those bands on it and have it tracked? No, the bird's perfectly free to come and go.

B   Do you worry?

A   About it getting caught by someone? Sometimes. Regardless, there's no choice. I couldn't put this bird in a cage. The bird would die. It takes its chances, like the rest of us.

B   I've never seen it, you know. Every time I'm here, the bird's out.

A   Strictly coincidence, I assure you.

B   Freedom is never a coincidence.

##

TWO PEOPLE WITH HORNS

A   You have no idea.

B   Really?

A   Of what it took for me.

B   You played the same note I did.

A   The same time, the same way. Don't you see?

B   I thought you had perfect pitch.

A   No!

B   You have a practiced ear.

A   What it took for me to be in the same place, to be almost the same person as you, long enough to play that one note!

B   You did all that?

A   Yes.

B   But we're so different.

A   Yes.

B   And then you had to get all the way back to being yourself again. To play the next note.

A   Yes.

B   What was it like? For that one note?

A   It was…a strange delight.

B   Would you do it again?

A   That isn't the point.

B   What is?

A   Sometime – when you're ready – I want you to play a note like I do.

B   I'm not ready for that.

A   I know.

B   But when I can.

A   Yes.

B   What was the transition like?

A   That I can't tell you.

B   I'll have to find out for myself.

A   Yes.

B   Is there any hurry?

A   To find out how we're all the same and all so different? Is there any hurry?

B   Let's pick up the horns again.

A   Who starts?

B   Play a note.

##

DIALOGUE FOR SPRING

A   Finally!

B   What?

A   Spring!

B   There's no such thing as finally.

A   After three hurricanes and four feet of ice?

B   You're so literal.

A   I happen to *like* daffodils.

B   So do I.

A   At least we agree about *some*thing.

B   It's this notion of finality you have. About spring. I mean, spring comes, spring goes. There's nothing final about it whatsoever.

A   I'd rather look at my purple crocus than split hairs about the philosophical nature of finality.

B   Then I can't help you.

A   I wasn't asking for help. I was rejoicing.

B   I don't rejoice.

A   I know.

B   It only sets me up for a pitfall. Sweating in summer. The air conditioner broken. What's to rejoice?

A   This.
        ##

BURNED

A   What's eating you?

B   I done been burned.

A   Funny, you don't look like charcoal to me.

B   One of those personal barbecues. No witnesses.

A   You're not planning on getting even.

B   Been a long time since I burned a bridge.

A   One of those suspension bridges made of rope hanging over the cavern?

B   Long way down.

A   Just at the last moment, the shirt sleeve catches on an overhanging twig, and the person is saved

B   Ask me if I care.

A   Little too early to turn the other cheek?

B   Already did. You ever hear of anybody with three cheeks?

A   So the twig snaps.

B   The twig snaps.

A   And this is not a cartoon where the person goes splat and springs right up again.

B   Splat. Period.

A   You don't by any chance want to tell me what this person did to you? Maybe get it off your chest?

B   Rehashing, I don't need. It's like that song, 'A time for love, a time for hate.'

A   But look what it's doing to you!

B   I'm preparing a special potion. I leave it at the person's doorstep. They stumble over it. They land in a pool of fizz. The person decomposes on the spot.

A   Where were you when the FBI was trying to get rid of Castro?

B   Busy being nice. It was taking up too much of my time I need for things like this.

A   Is this one of those theories about how we need enemies?

B   This is not theory; this is practice.

A   You're not actually going to do something stupid.

B   No.

A   What are you going to do?

B   Single out, one by one, the controlling types in this world.

A   And?

B   Let them hang themselves by their own rope. Because who needs their bossiness. Their hidden agendas, their self-serving "help"?

A   And how are you going to get people to see all that?

B   One of those 24 hour-a-day cable tv shows.

A   I presume you have a name for this show?

B   Yes: "TWO FACE". One talking head, two faces. Cuts down on hiring costs.

##

COUCH

A   There are still a lot of things I want to do.

B   What's stopping you?

A   Don't seem to have that old get up and go.

B   Maybe it's the change of seasons.

A   Or getting old.

B   C'mon.

A   It's not apathy. Because I still care about caring.

B   I wouldn't worry about it.

A   But day after day? It's a chore to get to the mailbox and back. I think about it, and I say, 'Too much effort.' This is no way to live. I have a flower garden to dig up.

B   Maybe you're going through one of those passive phases where it's o.k. to lie around. Maybe you're building up to something.

A   You think so?

B   Remember how you slept for a week and then built that laser beam condenser in two days?

A   And then collapsed for another week.

B   Maybe it's your bio-rhythms.

A   Would a bio-rhythm have a difficult time getting off the couch?

B	It could be a very comfortable couch.

##

KOI

A   What did you say you went to today?

B   A fish show.

A   A what?

B   The MidAtlantic Koi Society Fish Show.

A   Koi?

B   Imported Japanese fish. Thousand dollars a hit.

A   For a fish?

B   Apparently.

A   What does it look like?

B   Splashes of brilliant red, oranges, white, black. If you're a pro, you know by the coloring which of fourteen kinds it is.

A   Do they jump through hoops?

B   They swim around in circular plastic tanks and get admired. They're born black. The colors emerge later.

A   How big are they?

B   Maybe a foot. The size of goldfish you see swimming in the lobby of the Hyatt.

A   Is that how you tell what level hotel you're staying at – if it's only goldfish, instead of koi?

B	No – I think it's that you'd have to hire a special chef to feed them.

##

OH, THAT

A   Looks like you've just been through a lot.

B   Been thinking about changing my life.

A   What's wrong with it?

B   I want to contribute more.

A   Oh, that.

B   What do you mean, 'Oh, that'?

A   You make a contribution with every brush stroke.

B   I know. But today I thought it had to be finding a chromosome, or a new brainwave.

A   What happened to you?

B   Five tequilas and sunrise with a neuroscientist.

A   And you were going to give up painting?

B   Thought maybe I could combine the two.

A   You and math? I bet you can't divide a fraction.

B   It's true.

A   Trust me. Things work out.

B   You should talk. You're a biologist who wanted to be a belly dancer.

A   True. I go into the lounge at lunch hour and shake it up.

STAR TREK

A   Quick!

B   Check the oxygen levels!

A   Oxygen levels functioning.

B   I think it's an interstellar meteorite path swerve.

A   There hasn't been one of those since the year 2071.

B   My pulsar confirms the read-out. Check the shields.

A   Checking. I show normal shield strength.

B   Increase shield strength to Code 7.

A   Code 7, and holding.

B   Sometimes I feel like I've been here before.

A   *Déjà vu?*

B   No – more like computer re-runs of "Star Trek."

SHUTTLE

A   Still hurts?

B   Yeah.

A   Bad?

B   Bad enough.

A   So give it time.

B   I don't have time. The space shuttle leaves tomorrow.

A   You're taking this one?

B   That was the original plan.

A   But you can't. Not in the shape you're in.

B   Who has to know?

A   The first anti-gravity whirl, and the whole ship will know. You can't do this.

B   I have till tomorrow.

A   Twenty-four hours? What are you going to do – time travel to a shaman, and take a mud bath with capricorn juice?

B   You never did have much faith in the cap juice, did you? Worked wonders for me.

A   And what if you don't get back in time?

B   Then it's a while till we see each other again.

A   A while? You mean several light years.

B   Am I any good to you the way I am?

A   You just want to hear me say it, right? You have the guts to time travel, even though you've been warned against doing it one more time, but you need to hear it from me that I'll miss you. Is that courage?

B   No. Love.

##

LETTING GO

A   The best way to let go of something is to let go of it.

B   Just like that?

A   Yes.

B   Over how long a period of time?

A   It depends.

B   How long?

A   Oh, days – months, years – or an instant.

B   Instant? How do you get to that?

A   Years.

##

TREASURE HUNT

A   So what did you do with the stuff that was on top of the mantel?

B   I put it away. An assortment of treasures, to be sure.

A   So why did you need any new treasures?

B   Well –

C   You need new treasures because…

B   Because you grow.

A   I don't understand.

C   Because your tastes change.

A   But if the old stuff was valuable enough to be a treasure, then --

B   Because the depth of beauty is what makes it a treasure.

A   I got that part.

B   So when what you once thought was beautiful, wears thin –

A   The what?

C   The depth.

A   You go to yard sales for depth?

B   A treasure is something that speaks to you.

A   If you bought everything that speaks to you –

C   That's why she only buys things with depth.

A   I thought we were talking about ducks.

B   That's how I came to *have* the ducks.

A   Because they have depth? What's so deep about twelve wooden napkin rings, each in the shape of a duck?

B   I saw three ducks in the shape of napkin rings at the first yard sale, before I got to her place, and I knew she'd like them, but I thought they were overpriced. So I didn't get them. I just told her about them. And then she said, 'Oh, here. I already have a dozen I got at another yard sale, and you can have them.'

A   And that's where the depth comes in? Of what – a duck pond?

B   Yard sales can nourish the soul.

A   I tried. You have to give me credit for trying. But I don't get it.

B   Which part?

A   About the stuff that was already on the mantel *before* you got all the ducks.

B   Oh. The old treasures.

A   Yes. I thought they meant something to you.

B   They do. But I got tired of them.

A   Well then, when does it ever stop?

C   You mean life?

A   What?

C   Life doesn't stop. For any one person, it does. But not on the whole. Not for billions of years, anyway, till the sun burns out. But who knows what we might have come up with, by then.

A   Now that had depth.

C   Like treasures.

A   People uncovered ancient treasures in Egyptian tombs. The tombs didn't have to be re-supplied with new treasures every other week. If it's a treasure, it lasts. If it doesn't, then it was never a true treasure in the first place.

B   O.k. From now on, we'll skip the yard sales, and go find a duck pond instead.

C   We could take the napkins, and wave them at the ducks.

A   In surrender?

C   No – to remind them to enjoy their freedom, in case someday they get turned into a napkin ring.

##

A Word with Dylan Thomas

A   Good evening, Mr. Thomas. If I might have a word with you—

B   Better to have a pint with me.

A   Not now, thanks.

B   What better time? Surely the light will fall and man will stand on his knees to look upon the next dawn, embracing the wonder that it came at all.

A   If I could pose a question or two—

B   Pose away. What are we if not knock-kneed supplicants to a world we cannot call our own? A world so fanciful as to resist the catapault, concrete barrier, raging fire. This world that calls hither and yet vanishes at our touch. Merely think of it; lie idle in one's summer, and chortle through vast winter. Only spring and fall lie in between, hovering, as one is like to know. What then, speak you as visitor, or have you come to stay?

A   Why aren't you happier?

B   A fair conclusion. Another glass will see me through til I can see no more. Blurry then, I feel my way, through damp, through cornfields higher than my stance, til once again I tumble down, mankind on my shoulder, the weight of it suddenly lightened by the streak of a mortar's shell. I'll have no more of war, bodies and stench. Happier, you ask? Why? Come, I'll see you to the dawn.

A   Thank you, Mr. Thomas.

B   The sights I have seen, the days I have walked. Let me have the drink, I say.

A   One last question. Why do you write?

B   For the love of man and the glory of God, and I'd be a damn fool if I didn't!

A   Thank you. And now we'll get on with the evening's proceedings.

B   Glory be, to you all.

##

(B's next to last line is an actual quote.)

SWIMMING

A   So did you go swimming today?

B   No.

A   What happened?

B   It was the first week of classes. I had to buy a recreation pass in the bookstore, and the line was way too long.

A   So you didn't go swimming.

B   No.

A   I heard that the Balinese do things differently.

B   Differently how?

A   Their approach is to maintain harmony at all times.

B   What does this have to do with long lines in the bookstore?

A   The Balinese have elevated the white lie to a form of social harmony.

B   I don't get where this is going.

A   If I expected you to say, 'Yes, I went swimming,' then you'd say, 'Yes, I went swimming.'

B   Why?

A   To maintain my sense of harmony.

B   You want me to lie about going swimming?

A   Only if I was Balinese.

B   But you're not. So is it o.k. if I just level with you and say I didn't go swimming?

A   I can feel the inner core of my harmony teetering already.

B   O.k. – so I did go swimming, the water was great, and –

A   But your hair's not wet, and you don't smell of chlorine.

B   It was a lake. And I had a bathing cap on.

A   Ah, yes. Harmony has been restored. There's just one other thing.

B   What's that?

A   Next time, could you skip a stone or two across the water, for me? Always liked doing that as a kid.

B   Now *that* is going too far.

A   Oh?

B   A white lie, o.k. Virtual reality stone-skipping, no.

A   What's the difference?

B   Between a stone and a virtual one?

A   You mean between a rock and a hard place.

B   No.

A You can't get stuck between a real stone and a virtual one. It's just not possible. Unless you were only virtually stuck.

B I was referring to the difference between a white lie and virtual reality.

A The difference?

B Yes. I'd like to know where you stand on this.

A I stand on…uh, tradition, and when the Balinese came up with this idea, there was no virtual anything. Things just were what they were.

B If things were what they were, why did anyone need the white lie?

A It was for days when the swimming pool was closed.

##

THE GOOD DOCTOR

A   (British accent throughout) Feet is it, you say?

B   I'm a podiatrist.

A   Stand on our own two feet – is that it, eh?

B   I take care of people's feet.

A   Stand on one, then shift to the other. Wishy-washy, that's what I call it. You take care of that, do you?

B   I see to it that people can walk, on their own two feet.

A   Get there on your own two feet, is it? I get it. A bit of the old confidence-building.

B   I'm speaking of the actual use of a human being's two feet.

A   Oh, I see. It's dancing, then, is it? Fox trot, two-step – watch you don't step on your partner's toes, is it? Ballroom dancing, then? I see.

B   I'm referring to the complex act of walking. People take their feet for granted.

A   Oh, I see. Bit of the old thank your lucky stars. Land on your feet. Just like a cat, is it?

B   The balance is extremely important.

A   Bit of 'don't lean too much on another,' then, is it? I get it. Stand up for yourself, then, is that it?

B   Podiatry, like any branch of medicine, is both science and art.

A   An artist, are you? Explains the paintings on the walls, doesn't it? Good with the brush, are you then?

B   I am a doctor.

A   A doctor? Oh, then it's sick feet you've been on about, is it?

B   If you want to simplify it that much.

A   As luck would have it, I've got a bit of the sick foot, and here I am in the right place, after all. Now what would you be charging, or could I interest you in a wee bit o' barter?

B   What did you have in mind?

A   A bit o' paper.

B   A bit of paper? What kind of barter is that?

A   A ticket for a bit o' theater. Do you like the theater?

B   Why, yes, but –

A   Because it's a bit of a horse show. And I play the rear end of one.

B   Step right up.

##

BACK ON TRACK

A   What are you so depressed about?

B   I took a wrong turn.

A   Oh?

B   Thought I could learn to design web pages on my computer. It's too much for me.

A   So don't.

B   I'm not.

A   So you took a wrong turn. Back up, and get on the road again. You had an idea, it didn't work out – and now you get going again. Where were you before the wrong turn?

B   I was going to learn calligraphy.

A   Beautiful.

                                                         ##

TRUST ME

A   What have you been doing?

B   Worrying.

A   About what?

B   Just about everything.

A   All the time?

B   Just about.

A   But it's such a waste.

B   I'm trying to stop.

A   Chicken Little lived a very small life. You don't want that. You want the expansiveness of the sky, the roar of thunder, and the still light of late afternoon. You want the wings of a falcon, song of a cricket, and the peace of a turtledove.

B   All that?

A   Why not?

A   I'd be willing to settle for a sunset.

B   Why?

A   It's already five o'clock, it's cloudy, and the sun shows no sign of setting.

B   It will. Trust me.

##

JACK AND JILL

A   Jack and Jill went up the hill to see what they could see.

B   That's not how it goes.

A   I know. I thought a new spin would be refreshing.

B   O.k. What did they see?

A   Very large magnets, drawing them ever closer.

B   Magnets? On top of the hill?

A   Yes. To attract the sunlight.

B   Are you sure?

A   Quite.

B   Is this a new theory?

A   Something had to draw Jack and Jill to the top of the hill in the first place.

B   No. They went to fetch a pail of water.

A   It doesn't hurt to vary things now and then.

B   Tradition has its beauty, too.

A   I get restless. So I change things.

B   Are the moments so dull for you?

A   I just don't want anyone breaking their crown.

B   So this is Accident Prevention Week.

A   Yes. And any tumbling will be done on gymnastic mats.

B   So you're looking out for others.

A   Jill was supposed to go for help, not go tumbling after.

B   You could join the Rescue Squad.

A   I'm not good in emergencies. I just think that if people are going to fetch water, they should do it on their own. Didn't Jill have anything better to do than go along?

B   Maybe she liked the company.

A   Face it, Jack was a klutz.

B   So this is about choosing your companions carefully.

A   It's the magnets again.

B   How so?

A   The sunlight drew them together.

##

MOONLIGHT

A   Somewhere in the moonlight I've seen your face.

B   This is definitely a pick-up line.

A   No. Really. I have recurring dreams, and you're in them. I'm sure of it.

B   This is getting spooky. I'll have to be going.

A   Don't you want to hear the rest of the dream?

B   Well, all right.

A   We're in a boat.

B   I don't swim.

A   I know. In the dream, I've spent all evening convincing you to come with me.

B   It wouldn't be safe.

A   I know. I teach you to swim with a life preserver on.

B   Am I a fast learner?

A   Reluctant at first, but then you get it.

B   And then we're on a boat.

A   A catamaran.

B   And?

A   I ask you if you want peanut butter.

B   This is your recurrent dream?

A   Yes.

B   And you always ask me about the peanut butter?

A   Yes. Do you like it?

B   What do I say in the dream?

A   That's where it ends. That's what I've been trying to find out.

B   If I like peanut butter?

A   Yes. I just want to know.

B   I do.

A   Thank you. I won't bother you further.

B   Oh? I was just getting into this.

A   Really?

B   Yes.

A   Well, can I buy you a drink?

B   No. I have a better idea.

A   What?

B   Let's find an all-night grocery store, buy some bread, find a bench and have a picnic.

A   So it's true what they say.

B   What is?

A	Your wildest dreams can come true.

##

A THEORY OF LIFE

A   Do you have a theory of life?

B   Do *I*?

A   Yes.

B   You mean like is man basically good, or not? Does existence function on a higher plane? Are we all headed toward an unknown life?

A   Along those lines, yes.

B   I like the blue of the sky, the green of the trees and the brown of the bark that blends them together.

A   Then what do you do when the skies are grey?

B   Wait for the sun to come back out.

##

HEADING HOME

A   Can you tell me how to get to Richmond?

B   Virginia?

A   That's right.

B   From Maine?

A   That's right.

B   Well, if I were you, I'd head south for, oh, two, three days – stay on good 'ole Route 1 – and then ask around again.

A   Thanks. But if you could just point me in the right direction.

B   Say, are you sure you're all right?

A   Yes. Why do you ask?

B   Most folks would know to head south.

A   I could explain.

B   Oh?

A   I was a bird, in another life. Migrated north, back down south, every year, up and back.

B   You say you were a bird.

A   Yes. One day my wings gave out. I landed on a ship's deck at sea, hit my head on the deck, came back as a person in this new life, and haven't been able to tell north from south ever since.

B   You hit your head.

A   I know it's a little hard to believe, but—

B   No, no. We all carry a burden. Now all you have to do is make a left at the next corner, then bear right, and that'll get you headed to Virginia.

A   Thanks.

B   Now it's none of my business, but what's in Richmond?

A   The old nesting ground.

##

RECLUSE

A   What would be the point of going?

B   We could see lions and tigers.

A   There are zoos for that.

B   It's not the same.

A   I'm not going.

B   You don't want to see Africa?

A   I want to stay home.

B   You're turning into a recluse.

A   I am?

B   I've noticed it creeping up.

A   There's a recluse creeping up outside the house?

B   Your shadow, maybe.

A   I go out.

B   Less and less.

A   I'm all right.

B   I worry about you.

A   Worry isn't good for you. It stresses your nerves and makes you forget how beautiful the days are.

B   We're talking about you, not me.

A   Are your days beautiful?

B   They have their moments.

A   Is that enough?

B   That's why I'm going to Africa – to spice things up.

A   My spices are in the backyard. I see light through the branches and it's a stained glass window. I see evergreen boughs and sometimes the needles fan out like bamboo leaves. I see the—

B   O.k., I get your point. Not all of us have such adventures that close to home.

A   I didn't, always.

B   Oh?

A   But lately I do.

B   You mean since you've become a recluse.

    ##

THE RIDE

A   I'm not sure I can do this, anymore.

B   Then stop.

A   Are you serious?

B   Yes.

A   We're in the middle of Kansas. If I stop now, we'll never get there.

B   But if it's too much, what's the point?

A   We're due there by six.

B   True.

A   So we have to keep going.

B   Not necessarily.

A   We'll be late.

B   And?

A   She's expecting us.

B   A little delay won't hurt anyone.

A   The last time we were late, Aunt Mattie had a fit.

B   Aunt Mattie's been having fits all her life. What's one more?

A   I'm pushing on.

B   No.

A What do you mean, 'no'? Whatever happened to responsibility, and obligations?

B Whatever happened to not pushing yourself beyond what you can take?

A It was your idea to bicycle here.

B And it's my idea to stop. Now, before you cross a threshold your system isn't ready for.

A You mean I could have some kind of amazing breakthrough?

B You take your chances. But if I were you, in the middle of Kansas, on an empty stomach—

A Some tornado of the mind headed my way?

B Could.

A Bring on the lightning, bring on the rains.

##

THE MEETING

A   I missed the meeting. How was it?

B   It was good.

A   What got discussed?

B   I don't know.

A   You weren't paying attention?

B   I kept looking at people's shoes. Velvety black, then a pair in jubilant black and white, and a third in chestnut leather. I couldn't take my eyes off them.

A   You spent the entire meeting looking at shoes?

B   Well, yes.

A   It's not a shoe committee.

B   I'd like that. We could talk about shoes, try each others' on, and say where we got them.

A   A shoe swap.

B   There could be ballroom shoes and ones for pirouettes, and fancy shoes instead of Easter bonnets.

A   But that's not what the meeting was *for*. I need to know what happened.

B   Some people took their shoes off – I remember that much.

A   I'll have to get the minutes.

B At one point, everyone was waiting for the other shoe to drop.

A The meeting was that suspenseful?

B It was, for the other shoe.

##

MORTGAGE

A   Long time no see.

B   Been to the moon and back.

A   No kidding!

B   One of those private space rides.

A   Cost a lot, don't they?

B   Spent my life savings, on one big joy ride.

A   Worth it?

B   I figured if I waited for everyday space travel, it'd be in someone else's lifetime. I wanted to get a scoop on things.

A   And now that you have?

B   I like it here just fine. The pull of gravity, the tides, the moon. Makes you appreciate what you have.

A   Just like 'My Old Kentucky Home'? Home sweet home. Home is where the heart is.

B   Actually, no.

A   No?

B   Home is where the mortgage is paid off.

A   And that, I take it, is here?

B   Actually, I took out a second mortgage so I could afford the trip.

A   The trip was that important?

B   I had to be the first on my block.

A   And now your neighbors have to keep up with you?

B   No; they just have to come to my rent parties.

##

HERE AND THERE

A   Sometimes the wildebeast demands to be fed.

B   The wildebeast?

A   Yes.

B   No way.

A   Sometimes.

B   The wildebeast fends for itself.

A   Always?

B   There's no such thing as a dependent wildebeast.

A   Oh?

B   The wildebeast has been self-sufficient for millennia.

A   So, uh, I guess whatever it was that came to my door last night wasn't a wildebeast.

B   A wildebeast came to your door? From the plains of Africa? You mean a stray cat. Or a possum.

A   No. It was the size of a cow, shaggy hair, and wide eyes that stared at me until I brought it some food.

B   What did it do then?

A   Finished off the food, gave a swing of its tail and was off.

B   To?

A I don't know. The next house, maybe?
           ##

WIND CHIMES

A   Today, just after the rain, I was taken by the sight of our bamboo chimes.

B   Where were you taken?

A   Out of the ordinary.

B   North, south, east?

A   To the land of breathtaking beauty.

B   Are we talking about another dimension?

A   Possibly.

B   Because when your breath is taken away, where does it go?

A   I couldn't answer that.

B   Maybe it goes to people who have trouble breathing.

A   They have oxygen tanks for that.

B   What was breathtaking about the bamboo chimes?

A   Their ultimate stillness, after a heavy rain and wind.

B   You mean they were just hanging there?

A   Yes.

B   Not even swaying?

A   No.

B   They weren't doing *anything*?

A   Not to the visible eye.

B   How could that be interesting?

A   It was a moment of genuine peace.

                                                                    ##

THE 4th OF JULY

A   So what did you do for Independence Day?

B   Went to a picnic. Got a recipe for cole slaw.

A   I like cole slaw.

B   The recipe calls for a half cup of sugar, but I'd leave that out.

A   A half cup of sugar?

B   There are sweet cole slaws. But I'd leave it out.

A   That's a lot of sugar. What else did they have?

B   Oh, beans, a mandarin orange salad, and some tuna stuffed tortellini. And you?

A   Me what?

B   How was your fourth?

A   We saw fireworks the Saturday before. Big crowd – about ten thousand, I'd say.

B   Not one for crowds, myself. Rather stay home, make cole slaw for twenty.

A   Threading our way through the crowd that night, around the lawn chairs and blankets, people still seated who weren't in any rush, kids with glow-in-the-dark necklaces, Chinese people with their kids and their beautiful language. A Muslim woman in her burka. Fennel cakes, grilled corn, ice cream. And then the parking lot.

Total gridlock. Cars – engines running – twenty-five minutes, not moving an inch. We just sat in our car, with the radio on, looking at the chaos. Fifteen makeshift lanes feeding into one. Cars every which way. It was other worldly.

Then all of a sudden, after forty-five minutes, the cars moved, a park ranger was directing traffic. Then we heard a car load of teenagers calling out, 'Watch out for people! Keep three or four feet apart!' They kept calling out, helping. We made an easy left turn, and off we drove, into the night.

B   You were part of something alive and bigger than all of us.

$$\#\#$$

TALK

A   Let me get this straight. You want to know when I last saw the Divine Mother?

B   Yes.

A   Well, for starters, I'm not sure what you're referring to.

B   The Divine in its female form.

A   That's a supposition.

B   What is?

A   That there is a Divine – supposition number one. That there are male and female aspects of it – supposition number two.

B   Everything's a supposition. You, me, my cat. We're afloat in a sea of suppositions.

A   That's a bit unsettling. As suppositions go. What do you hold onto in this ocean you mention? A piece of driftwood? A raft?

B   The Divine.

A   Now we're going in circles.

B   That would be an eddy.

A   An eddy? In the ocean?

B   It's nature's symbol of going in circles instead of with the flow of the current.

A   I've always been one to swim upstream.

B   Watch you don't snag on a submerged log.

A   I keep a good lookout.

B   The Divine is looking out for you, whether you believe in it or not.

A   And I'd be ungrateful not to be thankful?

B   The Divine isn't looking for your gratitude.

A   Then I can about go about my business, as I was.

B   You'll never be the same.

A   Oh?

B   Because we've had this conversation.

A   Yet another supposition.

B   You don't think that everything changes?

A   And yet another.

B   What do *you* hold onto, may I ask?

A   Supposing that I hold onto any one thing. My life is kaleidoscopic; I hold onto whatever carries me across the sky. A bird, a cloud, the wind.

B   Supposing there are such things as bird, cloud and wind.

A   Yes. Supposing there are.

##

STARBUCKS

A   So how was your weekend?

B   We dodged the sun.

A   You found shade?

B   We found a free rock concert in the park. Middle-aged guys doing Jimmi Hendrix songs.

A   In the park.

B   Yes. Then we went and sat by the lake, watched some kayakers. It was peaceful, a little lonely.

A   But you were with someone.

B   Yes.

A   And it was still lonely?

B   Other people were walking around in groups of five and six. People from India, laughing. Families. Two year-olds. Eighty year-olds. I felt alone.

A   You haven't been alone until you've sat on a park bench when it's just you. Those park bench blues start closing in. Nobody seems to notice you; everybody passes on by. That's lonely.

B   Sounds like fortitude, to me. The drive to get out of your apartment, out to the park, on the off chance you'll meet someone. Or at the very least, have a change of scene. I admire that. Like the people who take themselves out to Starbucks on a Saturday night, nurse a latte through a pile of magazines.

A   I've done that.

B   Have you?

A   There's a freedom to it – knowing you can come and go purely at your leisure. Try it sometime!

B   I might. Some night when there's a ballgame I don't want to go to and I'm home alone.

A   Or call me.

B   About what?

A   We could go to Starbucks.

##

SHAPE SHIFTERS

A   So what's bothering you?

B   I used to be such a self-starter.

A   And?

B   Now I just lie around until someone else suggests something. And even then, I'm only half enthused.

A   How long has this been going on?

B   It feels like years.

A   Does it?

B   Years ago I had my astrology chart done, and the reader said the gods were—

A   The gods?

B   Or some such. The part I remember was about how they were—

A   Who is 'they'?

B   I have no idea. The point was that a railway car was going to run me over, and then just to make sure the job was done, the railroad car would back up and run me over again.

A   That's on the grim side.

B   And now I think railway cars come in all shapes and sizes.

A   Shape shifting railroad cars?

B   In the form of running over my spirit.

A   Flattened out, like a pancake?

B   I have no oomph.

A   Who says only railroad cars can be shape shifters?

B   I don't get your point.

A   A pancake could be a shape shifter, too. It could take off, like a flying saucer.

B   And do what?

A   Fly. Out from under the wheels of the railroad car.

B   A flying pancake?

A   Why not?

B   (thinking it over) Shape shifting…I like the idea – thanks!

##

RESTING

A   What did you do in meditation group last night?

B   We read a passage from the *I Ching*.

A   On?

B   Renewal. Health after sickness. Rest. Not shooting your wad after you have just a little energy built up.

A   Not depleting yourself.

B   Yes.

A   What are you supposed to do with yourself while you're resting?

B   Rest is self-contained.

A   No; rest is boring.

B   Boring is a stage of healing. It means you're not quite done resting.

A   Or that you've rested too much and it's time to get on with life.

B   That's pushing yourself. It'll get you back to depletion.

A   No. It'll get you going again. Like a good kick in the butt.

B   A premature kick in the butt will set you back.

A   Is that what it says in the *I Ching*?

B   It's open to interpretation. But it's ancient wisdom, so I wouldn't mess with it.

A   Since when does questioning something count as messing with it?

B   I meant to treat it with respect.

A   O.k. I respectfully question the *I Ching*.

B   What did *you* do last night?

A   Oh, nothing really.

B   You rested.

A   I took it easy.

B   You're constitutionally incapable of agreeing with me.

A   Possibly.

##

ODE TO JOY

A   Oh joy.

B   In what?

A   Oh joy of the days.

B   What about the nights?

A   Oh joy of the nights.

B   Based on what?

A   Joy of each breath.

B   Breathing is joyful?

A   Joy of sight, sound, the garden of senses.

B   I don't get it.

A   There's nothing to get.

B   Then why such joy?

A   There's no why.

B   Then where does it come from?

A   From joy itself.

B   Where do you find it?

A   Everywhere but evil.

B   I guess I'm stuck.

A   C'mon – I'll take you for a ride.

B   Where to?

A   The present.

B   That's where I'm stuck.

A   No; you're stuck in the past.

B   True.

A   So the more present you are, the less stuck you are.

B   The more present I am, the less stuck I am.

A   Yes.

B   Is that like a mantra – I should chant it over and over?

A   No – you might get stuck in the chant.

B   Do I have to do something novel every minute to stay in the present?

A   Moderation in all things.

B   What about evil?

A   What?

B   You're in favor of a modicum of evil?

A   The world is a balance of opposites, very out of balance at present.

B   And in the rest, you find joy?

A   In the rest and the doing, both.

B   You play with me.

A   With joy.

##

NICHE

A   I heard live Indian music tonight. A tabla player and a guitarist, who made the guitar sound like a sitar. The musicians are both Western. Then the tabla player did a duet with one of his students, who is Indian.

B   So you had a Westerner teaching an Indian how to play Indian music?

A   Yes.

B   Wherever people find their niche is fine.

A   I was thinking of taking up cake decorating.

B   Oh?

A   In Buffalo, you could watch the cake decorators at work in a supermarket's front window.

B   Working in a fishbowl.

A   I once knew a surgeon who decorated cakes as a past time, with all the precision of wielding a scalpel.

B   Nerves of steel.

A   But then there's all that sugar.

B   It's a thought.

A   So maybe that's not my niche after all. One time at a party, I met a man who was an expert in refrigeration. That was all he talked about, and people admired him for his expertise.

B And?

A I talked to a plumber. He said being a plumber was more dangerous than being a policeman, because sometimes people use Draino without telling him, and he gets burned.

B What does this have to do with Indian music?

A Well, there are morning ragas, and evening ragas. And you have to know which is which. Otherwise you could play the wrong one and upset people's harmony.

B Which relates to what?

A Too much sugar upsets the body's harmony. Too much refrigeration uses up more energy. Not all plumbers are happy.

B Who said they—

A So a niche is not necessarily a good thing.

B How did you—

A A person can get bogged down in a niche. Without one, you can be free-floating, open to whatever comes along.

##

ELEPHANT

A   I know what I want for Christmas.

B   Oh?

A   I want an elephant and a balloon.

B   I'm sure we could manage the balloon.

A   What about the elephant?

B   Where would we keep it?

A   In an elephant house. Like a dog house, only bigger.

B   Is this one of your impulses, or have you been wanting an elephant for some time now?

A   I thought of it three hours ago.

B   And it's lasted?

A   Yes. So it can't possibly be impulsive.

B   Were you thinking of a baby elephant, or full grown?

A   Full grown. They stay with their mothers a long time, don't they?

B   A full grown elephant in the back yard.

A   It won't bother the neighbors.

B   What about when it trumpets?

A   I'll keep it happy with lots of peanuts.

B   Getting back to the balloon.

A   Yes?

B   I don't mean to burst your bubble, but we're not getting an elephant, even if we could afford one.

A   No?

B   No.

A   Then don't be surprised if you wake up some morning and I've run away with the circus.

B   All this in only three hours?

A   I'm trying to make the most of each moment. Seize the day. Live life to the fullest.

B   How about if we go to the zoo and *look* at an elephant?

A   It's not the same.

B   We'll look at an elephant *and* I'll get you a balloon.

A   The art of compromise.

B   It's the best I can do.

A   (sigh) No one gets everything. Is that it?

B   Yes. But I understand the used balloons from the Macy's parade are up for grabs. Would you like one?

A   No.

B   No?

A   I only want one round balloon on a string, to remind me that I can float.

B   Then what was the elephant for?

A   I didn't want to be the only one with big ears.

B   Your ears are fine.

A   People tease me.

B   About your ears?

A   Yes.

B   What were people going to say if you had an elephant?

A   It would take the attention off me, and onto the elephant.

##

ECLIPSE

A   You can come over, but I'm in an eclipse at the moment.

B   An eclipse?

A   Things are dark. Tsunami, flood, earthquake. I think the gods are angry with us.

B   The gods?

A   Yes.

B   No one believes in angry gods anymore.

A   I'm beginning to.

B   There are scientific explanations for all these events.

A   Science doesn't acknowledge anger.

B   So you think Zeus is up there throwing lightning bolts?

A   Yes.

B   This could get you labeled as a crackpot.

A   I could also be right.

B   The Weather Channel isn't going to hire you to sit there and talk about angry gods.

A   I don't want to talk about them; I want to appease them. Before it's too late.

B   Is this the Apocalypse?

A   I didn't say it was the end. It's more like a warning.

B   Maybe you need a vacation.

A   That's the whole point.

B   What is?

A   There's no place to run to. We're on planet Earth and we're cornered.

B   What about Longwood Gardens? Or Great Adventure? Or Niagara Falls?

A   Running does not appease the gods.

B   Pretty soon you'll have us back to human sacrifice.

A   No.

B   What, then?

A   If we each planted a beanstalk.

B   You mean for the carbon dioxide.

A   No.

B   Beanstalks? To replace the rain forests?

A   No. To reach to the sky with a message on the tip of each one.

B   And your message is…?

A   'Don't give up on us – we're still trying.'

##

WINDOWS

A   I'd like you to clear your schedule for a conference call.

B   What are we going to talk about?

A   That's open-ended.

B   Open-ended. You mean there's no topic?

A   That's right. Whoever throws their hat into the ring first, that's what we go with.

B   Anything?

A   Yes.

B   I don't get it.

A   There's nothing to get.

B   My windows need replacing. We could start with that?

A   Yes.

B   My windows at home, I'm talking about.

A   Yes.

B   Let me get this straight. You need me on a conference call with – how many others?

A   Five.

B   Six of us talking with no agenda.

A   Right.

B   Is this some kind of social experiment?

A   We need to take each other as we are, with no set agendas.

B   Why would anyone care about my windows?

A   I don't know. It's a chance you take.

B   I might as well be interested in what the person in front of me at the deli line is ordering.

A   It might be something you never tried before, and next time you will. You might like the sound of the person's voice. You might strike up a conversation.

B   I already know these people.

A   Do you?

B   I've worked with them for long enough.

A   Have you?

B   What are we running here – a sensitivity group? How is any work going go get done around here?

A   Sometimes I think it's the only work to do.

B   Oh?

A   Finding some way to get on with each other.

B   I wouldn't invite some of these people to lunch, let alone to see my windows.

A   Exactly.

##

RETREAT

A   What have you been doing?

B   Reading *A History of God*.

A   Oh?

B   All this bloodshed, over an idea.

A   We got past human sacrifice.

B   Yes. And no. The suicide bombers. It goes on and on.

A   You sound world weary.

B   Yes. I am.

A   Maybe time for a retreat?

B   Yes.

A   I happen to be in the retreat business. We offer custom-tailored retreats. What would you like?

B   Trees. Music. Sunlight.

A   The trees and the music we can guarantee. The sunlight?

B   Two out of three is good.

A   As a batting average, two out of three is *very* good. Considering that all three would be perfection, which is a lot to ask.

B   I'm interested.

A   That was trees, music, and sunshine, right? Do you mind the rain?

B   Rain, fog, thunder – anything but what I'm in now.

A   Time.

B   Excuse me?

A   We'll throw in time with the package. You can use it any way you want.

B   Ahh, yes. A drop in the bucket as far as the millennia are concerned, but a lifesaver for me.

A   That comes with the package, too.

B   What does?

A   Forgetting about the millennia.

B   Oh?

A   We lighten your load.

B   Where does it go?

A   Where does what go?

B   When you lighten my load, where does the heaviness go?

A   Ahh. Now I see.

B   See what?

A   Where your heavy burden comes from.

B   Where?

A   From asking questions like that.

B   You can give me a rest from that?

A   Yes.

B   Sign me up.

##

TURKEY TALK

A   Sometimes even a wishbone won't tell you the truth.

B   You believe in wishbones?

A   Yes. But they're unreliable.

B   How can you believe in something if you think it's unreliable?

A   Wishbones can make mistakes, too – just like the rest of us.

B   Marrow and tissue, blood and waste, all trying to read the map.

A   And sometimes getting lost. Even if they've been there before. Or, as likely as not, new cells, first time out.

B   Then the question is who's reading the map for whom? Or is there a map at all? Maybe there's only routine, and sometimes a falling asleep at the wheel.

A   It's a lot of weight on one fragile wishbone. That's why I've invented a Zen wishbone.

B   A Zen wishbone?

A   Yes. Whatever you wish for, you get.

B   What's the purpose of breaking the wishbone at all, then, if you're going to get your wish either way?

A   It's the act that counts.

B Whatever happened to 'It's the thought that counts?'

A The thought has to be definitive. Getting to that point is an act.

B Unity of thought and action.

A Yes.

B And that's a Zen wishbone?

A No duality. The oneness of thought and action.

##

SMALL TALK

A   Somebody quick save the watermelons!

B   Is there a drought?

A   The melons have lost their sense of purpose.

B   How can you tell?

A   They're just lying there.

B   That's what watermelons do.

A   They're not growing.

B   Maybe they're on a plateau.

A   The garden is level. I think they need a boost.

B   Such as?

A   Could you just talk to them?

B   Me? Why not you?

A   A new face might help.

B   What do you want me to say to them?

A   Just make small talk.

B   With a watermelon?

A   Yes.

B   Such as?

A Well, talk about the weather. The height of the corn. Strawberry season. Give them something to look forward to.

B So you can eat them.

A Yes.

B Maybe that's exactly why they're stalling. Wouldn't you?

##

DHARMA

A   You were invited to what?

B   A meditation group.

A   It almost seems silly to ask, but what do you do?

B   The leader talks first. It's called a dharma talk.

A   What's a dharma talk?

B   I could give you an example.

A   O.k.

B   A talk about getting past the ego.

A   Why would you want to do that?

B   So you can transcend the self.

A   But then there wouldn't be any self left.

B   That's the idea.

A   But who would be standing here?

B   Excuse me?

A   I'd be talking to myself, in which case I'd be crazy.

B   You get past yourself.

A   Then neither of us would be here.

B   We'd evolve to some higher state of being.

A   We wouldn't exist. Is that your idea of a good time?

B   We'd be something unimaginable.

A   Whatever happened to 'if you can think it, you can do it'?

B   Isn't that a Nike commercial?

A   Is this a dharma talk?

B   Let me give you another example.

A   Are we back to where I exist?

B   Say it was a talk about your inner critic.

A   My inner critic exists, but I don't?

B   How would you silence the inner critic?

A   If I transcend myself, do I take my inner critic with me?

B   This is just an example of what a dharma talk can be about.

A   Isn't it in the Constitution, about the freedom to assemble?

B   Yes. And?

A   Don't we as selves have the right to assemble, along with our inner critics?

B   We get past self and inner critic, both.

A   Then there are no selves to assemble. What about the stuff in mail order catalogs that says 'some assembly required'?

B   Excuse me?

A   You have to exercise your rights to keep them. It's like going to the gym. Use it or lose it.

B   Transcendence is the most democratic gig going. You can do it anywhere – in the Congo, or in China, or—

A   You have to have the right to assembly in order to have the dharma talk in order to transcend it.

B   Right.

A   So be thankful.

B   Maybe you'd like to come to this group?

A   No; I'm too full of myself.

##

A POCKET

A   I hear you went to see the Dalai Lama.

B   Yes.

A   What is he, anyway?

B   You could call him the high priest of Tibetan Buddhism.

A   You're one of his followers?

B   I wanted to hear what he had to say.

A   So what did he say?

B   That war is an outdated concept.

A   O.k. What else?

B   That there will be peace in this century.

A   For certain?

B   He doesn't have a crystal ball.

A   I guess not.

B   He was also very good at saying, 'I don't know.'

A   There's a lot I don't know, either. Could I be the next Dalai Lama?

B   He was chosen when he was two.

A   So it's a little late for me.

B   You could still give talks.

A   Who would listen?

B   That's the whole point.

A   What is?

B   That 36,000 people showed up to listen.

A   A little pocket of sanity.

B   Yes.

##

LOGIC

A   When did the jellyfish sing to the moon?

B   When did the jellyfish sing to the moon?

A   Yes.

B   Is that a question?

A   Yes.

B   Isn't the question 'whether' the jellyfish sang or not, rather than when?

A   I guess it depends on how you look at it.

B   At what – the moon, or the jellyfish?

A   The question.

B   You can't look at a question.

A   Excuse me?

B   A question is a concept. An idea. You can't look at it. You can look at the moon, though. Or a jellyfish. And lots of other things.

A   But you could hear the singing.

B   What singing?

A   The jellyfish to the moon.

B   How would you know it's the moon they're addressing?

A   That's a good question. I suppose the moon would react in some way. Wouldn't you, if a jellyfish sang to you?

B   How would I know?

A   Know what?

B   If the jellyfish was singing to me? It could just as well be singing to the moon.

A   My point exactly.

##

TEA

A   I'm really sorry, but I just broke your favorite mug.

B   That's too bad.

A   It's in smithereens; I can't fix it.

B   That's all right.

A   You're not mad?

B   I'm practicing non-attachment to things.

A   Is this like when people start giving away all their stuff?

B   No. It just means we have other mugs to drink out of.

A   Well, thanks for being so reasonable.

B   Just try to be a little more careful next time, o.k.?

A   Is this the part where I get chided?

B   No. This is the part where you make me a new cup of tea.

A   I can do that.

B   Good. Then all's well in the kingdom.

##

THE LOOKING

A   So how was the crafts show?

B   Gorgeous!

A   What did you see?

B   Woven wire baskets, interlocking pottery bowls like lotus flowers. Beaded vases and shoes.

A   Shoes?

B   Yes. High-heeled shoes covered in beads.

A   Did you buy anything?

B   It was way out of my price range.

A   That's depressing.

B   No. I just pretended I was in a museum. I browsed to my heart's content, and came home with a head full of beautiful images.

A   A place you can go when the rest of the world seems so ugly.

B   Does it?

A   To me it does.

B   But look around you. The trees, the blue and white of the sky; it's a show you don't even have to pay admission to.

A   But then there's the news. It's so depressing. You listen to it, don't you?

B   Yes. But I also listen to the Earth, to the roar and calm of her oceans, the wind through her pine trees and the crackling of leaves underfoot.

A   That makes up for all the dead and wounded?

B   No.

A   Then what do you mean?

B   That beauty saves us, wherever you find it.

A   Then I'll look, harder.

##

THE NEW YEAR

A   It's almost 2010!

B   Already?

A   Where have you been?

B   Hiding under the couch.

A   C'mon.

B   No, really. I listen to the news, check the weather, and then I go for the couch.

A   You said 'under.'

B   Yes.

A   Only cats hide under the couch, when there's thunder.

B   A coal mine collapses in China. A suicide bomber pops off in Kabul. Someone buys an AK47. Believe me, the couch is the safest place.

A   I thought the idea was to take *part* in the world, to make it a better place.

B   I *am* taking part. I do the cowering. Someone has to.

A   We're not supposed to give in to fear. That's when the enemy wins.

B   It's nice under the couch.

A   Wouldn't you rather see the sun?

B   My cheek nestles right up against the carpet.

A   What about the soft white light of a late afternoon? Wouldn't you like to see *that*?

B   I would. But—

A   But what?

B   Couldn't I wait til the New Year?

					##

THRILL

A   So what did you do today?

B   Went shopping.

A   Oh? What for?

B   Because there was nothing else to do.

A   I meant, what were you looking for?

B   Something to fill the nothingness.

A   I meant like shoes, or clothes, or—

B   There was a blouse I didn't get.

A   Why not?

B   It was bold.

A   Bold is good.

B   Too bold. But I have buyer's remorse.

A   I thought you said it was too bold.

B   I did. But I liked it. For cooler weather. I might go back. If it's still there.

A   If you liked it that much.

B   I'm not absolutely in love with it.

A   But it's your anniversary!

B   It's more your kind of thing.

A   Bold?

B   Maybe I'll go back this evening. It's kind of a long drive.

A   How long?

B   Half hour. One way.

A   But if you really like it.

B   I could go ahead and be bold.

A   Why not?

B   I don't have anything really bold. Or maybe it's just something to latch onto. A craving. Like chocolate.

A   Chocolate is good.

B   As a treat.

A   That's what the blouse would be. Why not treat yourself?

B   You're right.

A   This is why financial independence is so great.

B   I'd still have to make up my mind.

A   Why don't you just get it?

B   I have a hard time making decisions. It must have something to do with confidence. Or perfectionism.

A   Or the thrill of the chase.

B People drive ambulances for that. Too much responsibility. Clothes are safer.

A When was the last time you had a thrill?

B Last night.

A Last night?

B Playing music with some friends.

A That was less than twenty-four hours ago.

B It's like playing a note on the guitar. The sound fades quickly.

A At least not all your thrills are material.

B Sometimes it's enough to look out the window at the evergreens. Other times – like today…

A It keeps the economy going.

B It's almost time to make dinner.

A Yes.

B The evergreens move so gently. And they wear the same green year 'round. Except when it's spring and the brighter green needles come out.

A I have to go soon.

B Maybe I'll go back tomorrow morning. The birds are calling now. And the shadows have fallen across my lap. Sometimes there are no sounds but a faint hum. Yes, I'll just settle back now.

A I'll be going.

B   Thank you.

A   And call me, o.k.? When you get the blouse?

B   The what? Oh, right. I'd almost forgotten.

                                             ##

DIALOGUE FOR CHRISTMAS 2011

A   Ho ho ho! So what do you want for Christmas this year?

B   Oh, the usual. Peace, joy, love.

A   Anything else?

B   Could that come with chocolate?

##

THE WEDDING

A   What are you so excited about?

B   I have a jazz gig coming up!

A   Oh?

B   A first.

A   Where is it?

B   A wedding. No money, but hey, it's what I wanted to be all my life.

A   A jazz musician?

B   Yes!

A   What are you going to play?

B   Old standards. Ballads. A little bossa nova.

A   Just you?

B   With a pianist.

A   You've improvised in public before.

B   But this is with a trained jazz pianist. It's not just New Age noodling, like I've done before.

A   I'm happy for you. Just don't get off track o.k.?

B   What track?

A   The deep sea diving.

B   Anyone can strap on an oxygen tank.

A   Oh?

B   But the jazz – improvising in the moment, the listening, the concentration, grooving with someone else.

A   It takes courage to dive. And skill.

B   Do you know how lonely the diving is? When you're down there, in another world, like an invader?

A   I thought you communed with the fish, and were awestruck by the coral.

B   It's dangerous.

A   Don't you go out on a limb with a flute solo?

B   It's not life or death. A wrong note, maybe.

A   So you have a life beneath and above water, both, now. And it's all about the breathing, right?

B   No one ever got the bends from playing the flute.

A   You're not thinking of giving up a livelihood because of one, non-paying gig? You don't even know if it will lead to something.

B   Who ever knows what something will lead to?

A   Spare me the metaphysics. What are you going to live on?

B   Oxygen. But not in tanks. And no more ropes to tug on if there's danger. I want to breathe my soul into the music and take my chances.

A   I hope this is temporary.

B   It's always about time: how many minutes of air left in the tank, and how many bars to make a musical statement in.

A   You're serious, aren't you?

B   I'm turning a corner.

A   I have to stand by and watch you make a mistake?

B   No; you can walk with me. You can even be my guest.

A   At the wedding?

B   No. The feast of life!

##

PAKISTAN

A   I wasn't going to read the article about Pakistani nuclear warheads, but then I did.

B   What changed your mind?

A   I thought I should know.

B   Why didn't you read it in the first place?

A   Oh, I thought it would be too depressing.

B   Was it?

A   Well, according to one Pakistani official, both sides are lying. That was depressing.

B   It's political maneuvering. Why would that surprise you?

A   I didn't expect such candor.

B   The unexpected depresses you?

A   No. The idea of nuclear warheads in the hands of terrorists depresses me.

B   There are some who say the world comes to an end in 2012, anyway.

A   An end as we know it.

B   Oh?

A   The end of an era. A Mayan era, to be precise. Which means the beginning of something else.

B   Such as?

A   Something unimaginable. Something magical. Something worth waiting for.

B   So the Pakistani warheads depress you, but the end of an era doesn't?

A   Warheads lead to destruction. A new beginning forges ahead.

B   How?

A   Gradually. Subtlely. Almost imperceptively. Like dew drops forming.

B   You're sure?

A   Yes.

B   This makes you an optimist.

A   Yes.

B   Then why do you have trouble getting out of bed in the morning?

A   That was before I read the article about Pakistan.

B   I thought it depressed you.

A   It reminded me to get out of bed and live. While I can.

B   While you can? That doesn't sound so optimistic.

A   Seize the day, right?

B   You mean, just in case.

A   Just in case what?

B   In case things don't work out so well in 2012.

A   Any day, every day, you never know what's going to happen.

B   And yet you're sure 2012 will bring good things.

A   In the long run.

B   And what about the short run?

A   Oh, the usual. More mistakes, history repeating itself.

B   And still something leads us out of the swamp?

A   Yes.

B   Sounds like a contradiction to me.

A   Yes.

B   And that doesn't bother you?

A   No.

B   You're awfully complacent.

A   I should jump up and down?

B   Don't we have to *do* something, to bring about all these changes, in the long run?

A   Yes.

B   Well, what?

A   Relax. And breathe.

##

CHEMISTRY

A   You know what I think?

B   Never.

A   I think all our feelings are chemical.

B   And?

A   So if we can just find the right formulas for peace and happiness—

B   I already have the formula.

A   You do?

B   Yes.

A   Where is it?

B   It's in your heart.

##

CHOPPING WITHOUT CHOPPING

A   What are you reading?

B   It's about *wei wu-wei*. (Pronounced 'way, woo-way')

A   *Wei wu-wei?*

B   It's Chinese. It means fighting without fighting.

A   Fighting without fighting?

B   Yes.

A   How do you do that?

B   I don't know; I'm only half-way through the chapter.

A   It doesn't make any sense.

B   That's because we're Western.

A   Fighting without fighting. You fight for a while and then you drop your sword?

B   I think it means you go with the flow of the battle, so you ease your way through the conflict.

A   The sword cutting water.

B   Yes.

A   Or separating air.

B   Are you sure you weren't Asian, in another life?

A   The transmigration of souls?

B   Yes.

A   Being born without being born. One soul effortlessly transmitted into another?

B   It would weave us all together, as one tapestry.

A   Except I don't believe in it.

B   Oh?

A   We only go around once. You either catch the brass ring or you don't.

B   I always did like merry-go-rounds.

A   Merrily merrily – life is but a dream?

B   I had a dream yesterday.

A   Oh?

B   I was in a log cabin, and I needed some firewood, only the ax handle was broken. Then a deer came, put its hoof on a piece of upright log, and it split neatly in two.

A   Chopping without chopping.

                                                       ##

About the Author

Judith's first novel, *Jigsaw*, was published by Macmillan. She is the recipient of an NJ State Council on the Arts Prose Fellowship. Her one-man play, *Birdland*, about Charlie Parker, was optioned by The New Federal Theatre, NYC. A one-act play, *The Sound of a Distant Drum*, was produced at the Princeton Arts Council. Her dialogues and poems have appeared in *U.S.1 Worksheets* and *Thatchwork*. Judith taught Creative Writing widely in the Princeton and New York areas. She lives with her husband and Hank the cat.

Made in the USA
Charleston, SC
30 March 2012